THE SUBJECT OF
LOVE
A Discourse

OGHENETHOJA UMUTEME

THE SUBJECT OF
LOVE
A Discourse

⌒

OGHENETHOJA UMUTEME

MEMOIRS

Cirencester

Published by

MEMOIRS
PUBLISHING

1A The Wool Market, Cirencester, Gloucestershire, GL7 2PR
info@memoirsbooks.co.uk www.memoirspublishing.com

The Subject of LOVE. A Discourse © Oghenethoja Umuteme 2014
First published in England, 2014

ISBN 978-1-909874-50-3

Unless otherwise indicated, Bible quotations are taken from the King James Version and
New King James Version of the Holy Bible. Scripture quotations marked with NIV,
are taken from the Holy Bible, New International Version, copyright 1973, 1978, 1984
by International Bible Society. All rights reserved.

Address all enquiries to the publisher;

Restoration Media House Limited +234-8101700665, +2348076190064,

Email: rmhltd.info@gmail.com

CONTENTS

Dedicated

To Umuteme Ewevino Princess.
Your charming smile sends joy into my heart always.

Love is described by most dictionaries as a strong positive emotion of regard and affection. Often this definition and widespread perception has made many see love as a deep feeling for the opposite sex, and as such many have learned to hate Love, as being the reason for their distrust. Many of those who seldom preach about it do so only as a means to extort money from others. Yet the Bible preaches that love would heal our wounds, and to ascertain this fact, God sent down His only begotten son as a show of love. What, then, is Love?

DISCOURSE ONE

"But Lord, there is still disunity in our families, the church and society. What could be wrong?" I asked in one of my meditations. I lay on my bed, waiting to hear a voice enveloping my thoughts from the Melchizedek Anointing Order. The cloud had gathered and the dark blanket over the sun was an obvious emphasis of the rain that was about to visit earth.

A little wind, should I say little? Maybe just a feeling of cool breeze, well, so it seems. Raindrops could be heard in the distance and finally the roof above me received its own share of the rain. Then a voice spoke to my spirit and my spirit informed me of what the voice said – "I rain on both the wicked and the righteous. My mercy endures forever. This is my character and anyone who wants peace must learn to become one who would show mercy always and always."

My spirit sent in another thought from my mind into the immortal realm: "What then is the root of mercy? How can I show mercy? I have heard the word "mercy" but what is mercy? I also know I am not supposed to be a hearer alone but a doer of what the Word teaches – teach me Lord, I want to know and understand what mercy is all about."

Everywhere seems to be silent. The rains have ended their drumming on the roof tops and the gushing sound of the accumulated flood pushes towards the stream down the slope. I had subtracted my thoughts from the environment to hear what the spirit said. In that spiritual consciousness, I heard in my heart: "Well said, son. The beauty of life lies in the essence of living. What are you living for? What would you stay another day alive on earth doing? Have you thought of this too? Don't worry, I am going to take you on a journey if you are willing, and as we walk I will take you into the heart of life, which will help you to know why there is disunity all over the world. LOVE! LOVE!! LOVE!!! And nothing but LOVE – This is the Essence of Living. Are you willing to learn Love? Follow me and I will teach you."

As I hear these last words, I sink inward, into myself, into my inner self and wholly subtracted from the physical. A light glows in the dark. There seems to be no life there and gradually, as if the earth is rotating faster than it ought to, I see the sun beaming. The rays are intense and create a warm feeling of joy in my heart. I sink further inward, deeper than before, and my thoughts will only resonate as fast as I can remember a succession of questions: What is love? Where is love? How is love? Who is love? Why is love? What is love? And they would repeat themselves again in these cycles. My ears and eyes were dead physically. I could hear nothing any more. I could see nothing any more. Was I dreaming? Maybe.

Into a garden of flowers, with streams running knee deep on a shallow rock bed. The water was so clear – and one could behold one's face as if standing before a mirror. I could see my face in the water. I cleaned my face in the water and dried it with a towel. As I looked more closely, there seemed to be a stain on my face. I cleaned it again with the towel and looked again – it was now clear.

About three metres from where I was, someone lay still and helpless. As I moved closer in my thoughts, I could sense that he was alive. "Help him to be like you" a voice said from behind. "Why should I do that? – I have only one towel with me and the soap I have here will only last till tomorrow" I retorted. "But you said you were ready for this journey" the voice replied. Must I share what I have kept for my personal use with another?" I explained. "Well you just lost the opportunity to help" the voice responded. I looked at the spot again where the man had lain, but there was no one there. "But Lord I cannot see the man, he has left all by himself!" I exclaimed. "Oh that! He was just an opportunity for you to experience peace and unity with God, but you just lost it" he replied. "No no no, it can't be, I must help him out" I wept bitterly, searching all through, in my thoughts, for the man, yet no glimpse of him anywhere. The lights that surrounded me suddenly started fading. Fear gripped my heart and I could see it panting in fear of being enveloped in darkness. "I want to learn, I want to learn about love" I said as I wept.

Then, suddenly, the light showed, brighter than the first light. I waited for a learning opportunity. Behind me was darkness, ahead of me was lit with a multitude of stars. I travelled through the path towards the stars in my thoughts, then I came close to a barrier made of sand dunes. They were seemingly growing taller as I watched. But any time I took my eyes off it and looked again, I would see it smaller than it had been when I first gazed at it. And when I began to focus on it, it would begin to grow tall again. While I stood there watching intermittently and getting filled with the experience I was having, the Voice said: "Nothing is there, you are imagining it all in your mind – move ahead and you won't see it again. The more you stay watching situations, the more they grow, but when you walk through them, they will never show up again". As I wandered, I couldn't link what the voice had said on the subject of LOVE that I was hungry to learn about.

DISCOURSE TWO

As I rode down the cliff in my thoughts, towards the edge of the sea with its beautiful blue waters, I was filled with joy, because I was about to discover the essence of living. A whale rose out of the waters like a huge mountain, and fear gripped me, in my thoughts. I prayed within me and the terrifying scene faded out of my mind. Nothing had taken my mind off the physical like this. It was time to discover life. I had had a dream where a widow smiled while gazing at me, with an obvious need for care. A popular Pastor who was also with me in the dream, told me this was his secret - having a number of widows on his payroll. They would only come and tidy up the compound, and that earned them care from the church. Is this Love, I questioned? No answer from my teacher. Maybe He didn't want to speak until I had filled my thoughts with several questions which would trigger the response from the Order - the Melchizedek Order.

My mind wandered again to a dream I had had some time ago

where another popular prophet had gathered people from all countries, paid their fares, kept them in a camp where they were fed, and then paid their fares back to their destination. And I asked again, "Lord, is this what you want from me?" No answer to my question. I sat wondering and looking uneasy. Then He spoke: "People need more than food to live. Money can buy food, but real love cannot be bought with what the physical mind can imagine."

I looked into a church, with fast growing members. And I asked – Lord, this church is growing so fast, what is the secret? He didn't wait for me to end the question before He responded, "You mean that church? You want to know what wickedness is? That is the best name to qualify the members – it takes a humble person like my servant there to pastor these people. They are wicked and greedy. They only want to answer to the titles of pastors, deacons and deaconesses. And my servant is aware of that, so he has allowed them to have their desire – to be called pastors of a large church. But their heart is the height of wickedness." This was around the 3rd of December 2013. I wondered, how can people grow so large with so much wickedness in their hearts?

"Oh! You still wonder why they are increasing. Now read my words in the scripture and you will see that when men gather in such multitude, they have never gathered because there is love in their heart." I quickly searched the scriptures and came across Genesis 6:1. Then I heard from a distance: "My servants worldwide are waiting for someone to hand over to, but they are not seeing anyone. Those who have been with them have been hypocrites all this while. They only saw my calling upon my servants as a means to their material ends. I would teach you, just be calm and follow me."

Below the cliff lay the sea, without end. The freshness here sent thrills of desire to explore the coast into my heart. I started my walk. Further down, as I walked, I remembered how Daniel in the Bible had walked by the river Tigris, and he was visited by an angel. I was prepared for the visitor who would take me on this journey, yet in my thoughts. I started sinking again into myself. I had just woken up on the 2nd of November 2012. It was 5:07pm, as I wrote on this day. In the dream we were waiting to have a full house on a fellowship evening. Two long whips were in my hands, one in my left and the other in my right. A pastor hugged me and smiled on seeing the two whips. Honestly I knew the two whips I had with me were sending a frightening signal to the congregation who gathered. "They are but sheep" the pastor said. "A whip sends fear into their hearts and they won't graze. Their inability to graze will make them look lean and they won't reproduce."

I woke up. A piece of paper lay by my side and a pen to write with. Right on my desk was my iPad. The dream was still alive in my memory. I took a little walk down to the church to search for a serene environment. I arrived at the church and went to the altar to pray: "Lord reveal yourself in this new book" I prayed.

With my iPad on my lap, I resumed writing. I was getting soaked in the billows of the Holy Spirit and waiting for my teacher to resume. Within this period, the thoughts to show that I care were ringing in my mind. First I decided to be close to the youths and go to rehearsals with the choristers. A sister was in their midst who had grown without the care of a father, but with her mother, as a single parent. I communed with my wife, as we needed to show her love as I would my own child. I became close to her, but it was not long before she misrepresented my closeness to her as desire to sleep with her, and she reported this. I was shocked! My heart gasped for breath and I wondered what had gone wrong with the human race that believers can't even greet one another with a holy kiss any more (Romans 16:16).

My teacher came in to say, "The breath you have in you today is a gift of Love from God". He continued, "You cannot live without it. Love can take you to any height of achievement in life. You are born with love inside you, but often humans lose it to the quest for territorial control. Even as humans grow in their family, there is this desire to be the most favoured in the home. And gradually, attitudes and characters that will make this manifest are practised and the parents fall for it, liking one child more than the others. This seed which was subtly planted by the devil will sooner lead to all manner of disintegration and suspicion, from the home, to the church and then to society. Now let me explain to you what usually leads to the kind of love humans do have - when you show likeness for anything and finally accept it in your heart, gradually you will develop a spontaneous love or false love for it. This act will render passive your active senses, which would have helped you to judge rightly. When this happens, you will discover that all your emotions are locked up in your quest to always have the thing around you. If however, someone points out a fault in what you had been loving and that fault gives you reason to reject what you had accepted, your active senses would come alive to help you analyse further why you should not have liked it in the first place. As this happens, gradually your spontaneous love fades away and degenerates into hatred. Now, let me explain something to you again. Humans are mere mortals who often think they have eyes to see, whereas they are actually blind. You would notice that the more they confess that they love, the more they find reasons to doubt themselves. Humans are driven by subtle emotions with selfish intentions. Human love can only strive on mutual benefit grounds, but it is not so with God.

"I am going to show you what love is all about. Now, imagine you are physically blind and told to make a choice, and after the choice you receive your sight and you now discover that your choice does not please you. If you continue to appreciate it, then you have the spirit of love in you. If not, you never loved. To be able to do this you need to discipline your physical senses to appreciate what your heart accepts. The human senses have a strong power of judgement. This is followed by the human ego and the thought of what others would say.

"Now take another instance. Imagine you are dressed up for a party and along the way there you find someone who is drowning in a muddy river and you have the ability to swim out and save his life. What will you do? If you leave because you don't want to get dirty, then you don't have the spirit of love in you, but if you go into the water in your clothes to save that life, then you have love living in you."

There was a long pause. My hands were aching. I sensed it in my spirit, and a vision appeared before me. I saw an old man leaning against a stick by the side of the cliff. His head was covered in grey hair. "What would that man be doing there?" I asked my spirit. I knew my teacher would pick it up from there and tell me why.

I waited for Him to resume His teaching, but He wouldn't say anything. It dawned on me that He wanted me to take a closer look at the old man.

The old man had a cloth about his waist. He leaned even further down on the stick as if he were in pain. "He surely needs help" I thought within my spirit. My teacher was still nowhere to be found. His voice had suddenly gone dead. My desire to learn about love was growing and burning inside me. Then ahead in my vision, slowly the old man walked towards the sea. I looked at him. Was he trying to take a bath by the side of the sea, I wondered? He leaned against the stick but he couldn't bend down. Deep inside me, I shouted, "he needs help, let me help him!"

"That is love" my teacher continued. "He surely needs help so that he would be clean. He needs food too, because he is looking weak also. Then he needs clothing to enable him to receive warmth."

Then I saw ahead of me in that vision, two images, with white linen, taking off the dirty clothes from the old man and bathing him. In a matter of minutes, the old man was looking like a young man in his early forties and he had a glowing smile and was rejoicing. "This is all God does daily" my teacher continued. "I am going to leave you with an assignment. You will go into the Bible and bring out scripture verses to support what I have taught you about Love as it relates to the character of God, and you will use this to teach others. When you call on me again to teach you on this subject of love, be prepared to show me evidence of how you have put smiles on others' faces."

After these last words, His voice disappeared and I discovered that I was the only one inside the church auditorium. My iPad battery was running low and I had to put it on the power source. Just as I did that, I heard: "That is Love, because you don't want your iPad to run out of power." I recognised it as the voice of my teacher, whom I thought had gone. I waited for His voice again, for minutes, then hours, but He did not speak again. Well, I have learnt enough and I have my assignments before me to do.

DISCOURSE THREE

My first check was to use a software search engine on my iPad to search for the word LOVE. As I did that, I remembered the parable of the Good Samaritan which Jesus had told His disciples. There was so much before me. The verses came rushing in and my meditation and grasping speed increased. Strength rushed into my veins. This must the Lord's doing, I thought within myself. I was full of energy to research and to desire. It went on and on, into the deep of the night. My eyes were shining, seeking to unravel every dot I came across. Voraciously, every word love represents entered into my heart and sat there.

And I saw – 'This is how you can show your LOVE to me: Everywhere we go, say of me, "He is my brother."' (Genesis 20:13). Here Abraham made a great demand on his wife – to deny her marriage and vows to show him love. My heart ached to see what human beings demands as a show of love. She would have to drop all the respect accorded her as a wife before the servants of Abraham to protect her husband, which meant that even if she wanted a hug from her husband, she wouldn't get it as it stands.

Again, this verse popped up before my eyes – *Then God said, "Take your son, your only son, Isaac, whom you LOVE, and go to the region of Moriah. Sacrifice him there as a burnt offering on one of the mountains I will tell you about."* (Genesis 22:2). I saw the heart of God here – we must sacrifice LOVE as a test of Faith. What a lesson! I imagined what must have being going on in the mind of Abraham. A son he expected for years now to be sacrificed as an offering unto God. In my mind's eye, I could sense his bones aching and cracking within him. I could hear the sob of his tears. I could imagine how he was going to deceive his wife or tell her the truth of what he was going to do with their only son. My mind wandered into oblivion. The thought took over my senses, and I began to appreciate what love means. It involves readiness to give out that which you had hoped for and prayed tirelessly for. Later in the chapter, God intervened, because He could see Abraham's pains yet ready to release. This is why God released Jesus Christ as a sacrifice for the sins of mankind (John 3:16), because Abraham had obeyed to give his heir as a sacrifice unto God.

Love brings comfort to us. This is what I got from this - *Isaac brought her into the tent of his mother Sarah, and he married Rebekah. So she became his wife, and he LOVED her; and Isaac was comforted after his mother's death* (Genesis 24:67 – *emphasis mine*). The more we brew the seed of hatred in our hearts, the more we will have discord. Isaac loved his wife, and he received comfort of her. This is lovely. It goes further to show that if we would just learn how to love, we would be comforted by the instrument of love we bear. It sparks joy and resonance of peace and tranquillity around us, and everything would begin to vibrate in resonance to our heartfelt love and desires. You want comfort? Then love the source of the comfort you expect.

I wasn't tired yet. I still wanted to learn more, and my eyes caught this - *Isaac, who had a taste for wild game, LOVED Esau, but Rebekah loved Jacob (Genesis 25:28)*. You are loved by people when there is something in you that would meet their needs. Is this love at work? But it is a fact among humans, as my teacher had said – we love for material gain. I felt really touched in my heart that humans have to love people conditionally. Even the apostle John said in 1 John 4:19 - *We love because he first loved us*. Can we love unconditionally? This is a question we must answer to know if we have the mind of God in us.

Further I read - *No one has ever seen God; but if we love one another, God lives in us and his love is made complete in us. And He has given us this command: Whoever loves God must also love his brother (1 John 4:12,21)*.

More verses I saw perfectly explained to me that the problem the world is facing is lack of love. There is no love anywhere. Now that I am through with the scripture searches and study, I would be carrying out my practical assignment.

DISCOURSE FOUR

I remembered some time ago a voice said to me, "the son of the neighbour near you has not paid his school fees," and when I did paid the school fees, though that was the last money in my savings, the Lord blessed me. The Lord had told me to attend to the needs of a widow and I went back to the Holy Spirit to lead me to the widow who will merit this love. As I drove by, the Lord said "Here she is." I alighted from my car and the voice informed me of the amount she needed at that instant. I obeyed and left.

Before this time, I was driving one morning in January 2013 when I saw a young lady with a child on her back. The Lord instructed me to park the car and walk up to the young lady, as she was in need. At first, she denied being in need. As I walked back to the car, I hear the Lord tell me to return to her. I was really angry with the young lady and said "Haven't you been disturbing God for help in your prayers?" She burst into tears – she claimed she had nowhere to lay her head. I told her to calculate how much money she needed and come over. She did, some days later, and I had to give her what she requested from my savings.

I was practising what the Lord was teaching me. But many didn't know I was undergoing training from the Lord. Within this period, so many people needed help. In some cases, a voice would tell me to proceed, in other cases I would be instructed not to bother, except I just wanted to be good, because the person wasn't sincere. I was invited to pray in a church and I made a pledge, and the moment I stepped outside, I heard a voice telling me not to fulfil that pledge because the pastor would use the money for personal gain and not for the work of God. In another instance, I was instructed to pay a certain amount of money into the account of a servant of God, and when I did, within that same period, someone also paid the same amount into my account as a seed offering. I then remembered when the Lord said – "Give and it shall be given unto you" (Luke 6:38). Should this be the reason why I must Love? I asked to know, but within me, my heart wanted to find the truth about Love.

I was getting hurt again by some of people I had been of help to. It became a sleepless night for me as they were not serious with the church teaching programs. I had many challenging what I was teaching with claims that they had been older Christians in other churches before they joined our ministry.

I prayed and wept before the Lord, and He said, "I would take them away from you." And before I knew it, they had all left rebelliously. And He said, "Now I have taken them away from you, if you bring them back again, you will have to struggle with whatsoever happens." The moment I heard this, it dawned on me that when we do things on our own without the Lord's guide, we may end up miserable.

My heart jumped for joy. I told my wife, "I am indeed happy today, because the Lord has taken away my burden."

In love, there are pains to bear, but in some cases, these pains become thorns in your flesh and you would want God to take the perpetrators of the pains away from you. Never drive people away from yourself, let the Lord do it Himself and this way you won't have any regrets for not loving your neighbour as you love yourself.

DISCOURSE FIVE

As I walked across the lawn, I came across two lizards which had entangled themselves in what looked like a fight. I stayed to watch the scene. "This is all humans do" my teacher said. "Sadly enough, the reason for their struggle is not really worth it. They struggle for women or men to have sex with, they struggle for position and fame, they struggle for food, they struggle for power. All these are enemies of love." His voice switched off as if there was a power failure. I reassured myself that I was ready for the discourse, because I knew that soon he would come back as a rain visiting the earth, with so much information to teach.

Before I could say "Jack", he was back. " I am going to take you on a journey" he said. "A real long journey." Right beside me was a wooden chair which is usually used in the kitchen for sitting. "Three hundred and sixty five days make a year and you would add one to it to make up the days in a leap year" he said. "Though this is human wisdom, it yet shows how man loves to keep every fragment of the day he has. For every second humans live on earth, so also they draw nearer to their graves. But often you would see people crying over a dead person, who obviously have been rejoicing for every new year he celebrated without the thought that as he celebrated, he drew closer to his grave, year by year. Do you love the grave? 'No' would be your answer. Is the grave inevitable? You would desire the rapture I know because you are a faithful teacher of the word. What would mankind be doing on earth without the show of love to one another before Rapture comes? Do you love the dawn of a new year? Of course you would answer Yes. But in that dawn your destiny is drawing closer to its termination. Do you believe this?" I nod my head in response. "Now," he continued, "In each of these, which would you say has to do with the demonstration of Love from God - the new days and years, or the inevitability of the grave? Now I will teach you. Love is all about accepting yourself where you find yourself. And if humans did this, there would be no need for envy. The act of jealousy kills the display of love. Jealousy is borne out of greed. How many humans would want to release a gift to their enemy that would cost them much pain? Yet this is what God does daily. The rain, the sun, the moon, etc are a show of His tender mercies.

"I know you would ask me again what tender mercy is. You see, long before the world came into existence, I was sent to fill the formless world with the heart wish of God. Was the earth friendly to me when I did that? No, it was a cold mass of emptiness. I deprived myself of the peace and glory I had in heaven to fulfil the heart wish of God for the Earth. Do you have that heart to sacrifice your comfort? Can any human claim to have done this without any physical reward? Even now I have been on this earth for years now carrying out the wishes of God for humans. Have you taken thought of that too? You see, greed is the heart of sin and this is what has filled the heart of man. Even the so-called men of God are greedy. They want fame, a name, wealth - Is this not true? Now let the Lord take away the physical blessings and the fame they are enjoying. Will they ever claim to be pastors? Check it. The facts are in the prayer points they make daily.

"Love is plain. It has the heart of acceptance. Have you not read in the scriptures that the greatest among you must serve you? Well, let me not bother you with that now until we talk about service. I want you to take this with you, that if we must love, then we must be ready to accept who we are and carry out the responsibilities apportioned to us without complaint, just as I have always done, right from the beginning of existence.

"Now you will go into the scripture to encourage yourself with scripture verses relating to how you can live a life without greed, envy, and contempt."

DISCOURSE SIX

I soliloquised. Did I? It was two thirty a.m. The thoughts of my earlier encounter with my teacher had taken over my reins. Yet I desired more. I was experiencing fresh dew and the anointing to succeed as a servant of God. My inner mind was beginning to accept my new-found life. I was changing inside. And I knew that to fully manifest what I was learning, I would have to carry out all the assignments. I brought out my Bible and prayed: "Lord lead me right into the verses that would add value to my study"

It was on the 19th of January 2013 when my teacher said to me "Life is made up of people on a race to nowhere, and as such they would always need someone to take them somewhere." As I got engrossed in His teaching, my heart became filled with words of wisdom and I couldn't help but just write down as they rushed into my heart:

■ Learn it well and you will live it well.

■ Live what you learn and you learn what life has to give.

■ Be what you cannot, and you have started the dreaming process.

■ Expect that some day you will walk in the cloud and you won't give attention to thunderstorms.

■ Open your heart to learn something of value every day and you will see eternity.

■ Bake a cake for a friend while you go hungry and don't expect a thank you from him/her, and you will see an endless smile on your face.

■ Occasionally beat your chest hard, and you will know how painful it is to trust in oneself. Lift your hands to God and you will see how free you would become.

■ Write your name on a ball and drop it in an ocean and never expect to see it again. Someone will pick it up on the shore some day and call your name.

■ Meet your enemy and tell him/her how his/her character has turned you into a better person. This is the last statement he/she ever expects to hear.

■ Sometimes claim to be older than you are and you will see people admiring you. Also sometimes claim to be younger, and you will see how much effort you have to put in to convince people that you really are. Taking up higher challenges always makes you admired.

■ Win an Olympic gold medal and keep it out of your sight. You will never dream of having another. Wear a gold necklace and you won't want to walk through a crowd. Imagine how successful you have become and you will see joy in your heart.

■ Bless the day you were born, and that day will keep on blessing you. Curse the day you were born and you will see your life withering, because you never existed as long as that day is cursed and everything cursed must die.

■ Tears attract sympathisers who often leave you with a hiss and a sad face, and will never wish to be what you are. Joy attracts everybody and some will leave you to tell the story with a smile on their faces, while others wish they are what you are.

■ Challenges are mines of hidden treasures. The harder you dig, the closer you are to triumph.

■ Everyone is a gold digger, it all depends on whose yard the gold is dug from. This is what distinguishes the accuser from the accused.

■ The poor sees the sea and watches the waves with surprise and fear. The rich sees the sea and prepares to put his bed on it so that the waves will toss him to and fro as a means of recreation. Success-driven people see challenges as recreational experiences.

■ The poor man says "I will go and see first before I believe". The rich man waits to hear the story from the poor where he sits and employs the poor man to keep on bringing him the story of what he sees daily. The poor man is glad to hear that the rich man is interested in what he is seeing. The rich man is also glad to have someone seeing for him. With time the rich man tells the poor man to take him where he goes to see, then the rich man gets there and sits down so that the poor man will have nothing else to see but his old rich friend. You can only become the success you dream of when you see the importance of getting value from the success stories of others and making yourself become another success story.

It was after this, I took notice that my teacher had been the one teaching in my heart.

DISCOURSE SEVEN

It was drizzling outside. I had vowed in my spirit not to allow anything to distract me from my encounter with my teacher as I learnt the essence of love.

"The world must experience Love" I commune with him in my heart. I knew that my spirit would soon inform my teacher, so I waited for a reply. The environment was noisy as people rushed in from their workplaces, for fear the drizzle would turn to heavy rain.

So I took my iPad and left for the church. Sitting on my usual seat in the main worship auditorium, I waited for my teacher. As I did so, I heard a voice: "Not today, you are going to sit on the floor if you want me to teach you." I recognised His voice. It was my dear teacher. I obeyed with tears running down my cheeks. "Humility! Yes, humility is all humans need to experience Love" he began. Why would humility solve the problem the world is facing? Very simple. It would make no one see himself or herself above another. It would bring equality in judgement and the allocation of resources.

Governments all over the world are cheats. Those who own businesses are also cheats. Even in the church, you have more cheats than faithful worshippers. People cheat even God in the repayment of vows. People give their spare time to God. These are the elements of pride. How many people do you really think obey the anointing you carry? Have you not been challenged over decisions you make? Now let me show you what would happen eventually as a result of pride, many people will be caught in the devil's snare because they won't accept warnings that would save their souls. Now you should continue to be humble and you also need to teach others how to become humble. You have too many proud people in your congregation. Your first duty will be to teach them to be humble. The moment the spirit of pride dies in them, they will see increase on every side. Send them the kinds of errands that would make them err, and when they do err, teach them and refer them to the scripture. Tell them to inquire from me, the Holy Spirit of God, what they needed to do and I will be glad to take them on a teaching journey."

As I wondered over this, I heard Him say to me, "Now I am going to teach you the power of positive Christian interaction. "You see", he continued, "Interaction simply means to commingle, no matter what your class. Negative interaction is characterised by gossip, hatred, stagnation, suspicion, fear of denial, intimidation etc, while positive interaction is characterised by trust, increase, help, love and the like. You may want to know why we need to interact positively. Well, here are some reasons:

■ To understand one another.

■ To build and foster unity.

■ To build trust - if we know each other's intention. You must understand that many live a life of disguise. So be mindful of this fact of life.

■ To create an environment for fellowship.

■ To obey God because He commanded that we should love one another.

■ And the most important is:

■ To build a relationship.

"Now I will explain to you the instruments you need for positive interaction. They include fear of God, love, humility and respect. When all these are done you will see the following growing in your life and in your neighbourhood:

■ Effective fellowship in the house

■ Forgiveness

■ Joy in everyone's heart as they rejoice more.

"People are unable to interact openly because of lack of trust and domination, which is the after-effect of an inferiority complex due to the fact that people do not have the same level of intelligence and wisdom, the same spirit and interest. You must know that many people come to church because they see the church as a means to an end. The church is seen by these people as a solution to their problems, spiritual and physical, and not necessarily because they want to serve the Lord. In effect, if they must serve the Lord, He must make their marriage desires come to pass, or provide them with a job. Within the church you would also see those who meant well - they want to build a God-fearing family, internal and external, that will thrive to succeed. These are the people who build a church. They see the pastor as their family member. So they ensure they support him and his wife. The women stand behind the wife of the pastor. The men stand behind the pastor. The youth flock around both, to ensure that the vision of the church succeeds. The problem you have been having is that you have too many sad people who don't see any reason to appreciate God. Remember the Scripture says "Rejoice evermore" (1 Thessalonians 5:16). Not that they are really sad because God is not helping them, but it is their character to be sad as if someone has collected what belongs to them. And as such they find it difficult to:

■ Glorify God.

■ Put their energy in the work of God.

■ To respect the Pastor and his family, and those in authority over them.

■ Love those who seem to be better than them.

■ Accept corrections.

"They are always looking outside to find a better place to run to. They are not ready to build and they cannot build with you. Put a round peg in a round hole and you will succeed and experience love flourishing."

"Now that you are doing well with this wisdom, it is time to learn how to live a life that will bless you. This is the first thing you must do," he went on. "When you pray, you share responsibilities – "God your word says..." - do this for God. You outline your own responsibilities, to obey and do His Command. Your neighbours have their own responsibility in that prayer if you truly love them. Let us see how this works:

■ You eat the wealth of the Gentiles when you serve God as a lover of salvation, that is, as the priest of the Lord - Isaiah 61:6.

■ Your enemies are at peace with you when your ways please the Lord- Proverbs 16:7.

■ The Lord anoints you with an oil of gladness when you love righteousness - Psalm 45:7, and so on.

"What then are you to pray for here? In each of the release and promises above, there are prayer points inside. Your prayer is useless when you don't understand the needful. It is from the needful that you apportion responsibilities.

"Your thinking is what makes or destroys you - *As a man thinketh so is he* - Proverbs 23:7. Meaning that the reason you are where you are is as a result of your thinking pattern. The more you think of godly solutions, the more you become wise in the wisdom of God. This is why you are here. What should bother you more is how to grow in the wisdom of God so that the beauty in His kingdom will visit you. This beauty of God is nothing but LOVE.

"How does God answer prayers? Let's see:

■ This is where many usually err - Isaiah 30:9-10,12: people run to fake prophets who dupe them because they are not ready and prepared to hear sound doctrinal teaching. Many parents did not learn about God on time and so the children grew with the wrong wisdom.

■ God then punishes those who had erred - Isaiah 30:13-14.

■ God expects that that they should return to Him - Isaiah 30:15.

■ But what happens is that many would run out to join the occult, meet fake prophets, etc. Isaiah 30:16.

■ The more they do this the more the enemies chase them and make them groan from the effect of pain - Isaiah 30:16b-17.

■ Some however pray that God should make things right, crying and repenting and interceding for others that the Lord might calm His anger - Isaiah 30:18-19.

■ The Lord will then lead them to a Pastor after His heart to teach them where they had erred, because these Pastors have become stewards of the mysteries of God- Jeremiah 3:15, Isaiah 30:20, 1 Corinthians 4:1. They possess mysteries that will turn lives around, and these mysteries are contained in what they do teach and write.

■ And as one hears the teachings one is supposed to build Faith in what they hear so that they would eventually recognise the voice of the Holy Spirit behind and instruct them on the wisdom they have consistently received - Isaiah 30:21.

■ At this stage all they need is to continue in the doctrine of their teacher so that they do not err against God until they can divide the word of truth by themselves - 1 Corinthians 4:16, 1 Timothy 2:15, 2 Timothy 2:1-2.

■ Then increase would come as they also begin to teach same to others who have come into the fold, because all who come in might be passing through similar situations as the one they have gone through. This makes all of them become one in flesh and spirit, knowing that everyone has gone through similar afflictions. No one should boast of his/her spiritual superiority. Our gift is to be employed to save others in the vineyard of the Lord."

From these teachings I was able to find out the problem with many of us, and why we are unable to experience the beauty of LOVE:

We have drunk the old wine - Many of us have heard so many preachers before who have taught us so many things and we take that doctrine and mix it with what God is doing wherever we go. If we take a look at the beginning of Luke 1:1-4, though Theophilus had heard of the word of the gospel, it dawned on Luke also to give his own account. And Luke would expect that Theophilus must read through with open mind. You must open your heart to learn what God is saying to you. I read a lot, and the Holy Spirit has also explained to me whatever I read. All I do is invite Him in.

For instance, starting a church is a good initiative by people who must be filled with the Holy Spirit to gather as one, but they often err in trying to get on with doctrinal theology instead of waiting for God to raise teachers for them. As far as I am concerned, every other thing can wait. Let us know why we are here on earth. A journey started in chaos ends chaotically.

Jesus started His discipleship with teaching - Acts 1:1. I am learning to live the life the Lord is teaching me and the information is contained in my books. They remain the only evidence of the teachings I have received. Let us endure. There is no need to be in a hurry. You are redeemed to redeem. You are born to save. Your being born again is useless until you are a blessing to others.

DISCOURSE EIGHT

It was early in the morning and my teacher was right here to teach me. "You remember the day you came to this altar to pray for God to touch your wife and the word of the Lord came to you that you should go back and love your wife? The problem you had was that you were listening to the voice of the culture you grew up in, which sees the woman as one who should play second fiddle, and as such you were not recognising her help in your life. Love grows in an environment of appreciation. Even in the church you don't expect people to be perfect overnight. The world has been through a lot of modification since creation. When man was in the garden, God gave him help. This is what appreciation is all about. When people receive a soothing sensation from others, they will put in their best. All over the world, the reason people don't see growth is lack of appreciation.

"Now I want to be very hard on you. Remember you called for this teaching and as such I am going to drill your heart so that you would be able to teach others with the same drill you had received. You are going to send messages of appreciation to everyone who works with you in the church, both those who had left and those who are still serving with you. Then you would encourage your members to appreciate one another and even their enemies. You can now go into the scripture to teach them why they should appreciate one another, those who lead them and even God. I am not talking about myself, because I know that you humans don't recognise me as often as you should in your daily lives and even in your gatherings."

I had gone into the studio to record the demo of my song, "We must show we Love." The lyrics go like this:

We must show we care
We must show we love
If we have the blood of Jesus in our hearts
We must show we love

As I became more engrossed with the subject of love and knowing that I need the Lord Jesus to live inside of me to enable me express love, I sang:

Invade my heart
With your love, so I can do the things you do
Invade my heart
With your joy, so I can be more like you Jesus
Invade my heart
With your trust, so I can defend your name.

This song finally matured into a hymn, which the Royal Diamonds International Church sings on Sundays.

The Lord was perfecting my ways. Why did I pray this prayer? The ways of the Lord are too mysterious for mortals to understand. There are many religious and occult gatherings all over the world that teach their initiates the subject of reincarnation. I have asked myself time after time why anyone would want to return to this earth the way it is now, without love and care. I am forty-one now and I don't see anything so fascinating about a world with war, pestilence, hatred, moral decadence, unemployment, social vices and the like. I would rather ascend unto God in heaven where I would live as angels do. This is the promise of love in John 3:16 – my soul shall not perish but have eternal life.

I once spoke with a member of a sect that teaches reincarnation. He claimed that departed souls return to earth to be given birth to by new couples, and my reply to him was that these returning souls are responsible for all the ills in society, because as imperfect souls which could not ascend to God, they are bound to perambulate the dark until they come to couples who have no Christ in their lives, and would use them as a medium to come back to earth to continue the acts of greed, gay marriage, lesbianism, kidnapping, assassination, money laundering, suicide bombing, etc.

CHAPTER THREE

If we grow in love, we would be sure of a resting place for our soul in the presence of God. Let's go for it – Love is the secret.

DISCOURSE NINE

I was getting tired, and the night was far spent. I heard the voice of my teacher, but I was too weak to write. "You don't want to write? Remember you called for this" he said. I looked at the clock - 12:30pm. But what would I do? My teacher was here already. "Love doesn't give up. Remember the principle of acceptance? That is what Love stands for. Your strength must grow by the day in order for you to sustain the demands that Love puts forward. You may not be willing to, but you have no choice. How many people have rendered a little help to others and would make so much noise about it? Well, many. That is what is wrong with humans. They easily get tired helping the same person over and over. When people make mistakes, is it not your responsibility to teach them and ensure they do not err?

"I guess I am getting on your nerves. But you called for this meeting. Love is dying daily in the hearts of men. I am glad you signed into this teaching with your might. I won't take much of your time but you should sit back and think about what help really is. If you love, you must help again and again. People have offended you even when you have sacrificed to help them, but you are a teacher of the word of God. Don't you know that teachers must be very patient? I am going to leave you for the day. Don't fail to call on me when you need my help. You must teach what it takes to be patient even when you have no reason to be."

On hearing this, I lay back on my bed and tried not to think of anything, because I know that if I ever do, my teacher will soon come back to explain. Then I slept.

The following morning, I tried to go into the scripture to prepare my note on patience so that I would teach the church. But the patience the church understands is merely about life challenges and not about how they would render help again and again to someone who had disappointed them over and over.

The first portion of the Bible that struck my eyes was on forgiveness. Now let's see the facts clearly stated here. Jesus gave the law in heaven concerning forgiveness, 70 times 7. But I wondered why Satan was chased from heaven if this law existed. I was very sure that Satan never repented of his sin against God. I knew that as a human, it would be difficult for me to keep on forgiving those who wrong me 490 times if we go by simple multiplication of 70x7. But, I remembered that the mercies of the Lord endure forever. If this is the case, why then would anyone go to hell for committing sins that are out of his control? Well these were just my thoughts.

As I meditated more, I saw John 16:8-9. The Holy Spirit shall convict the world of sin, and sin is explained to mean not believing in Jesus Christ as the mediator between sinful mankind and God, the creator of heaven and earth.

DISCOURSE TEN

I tried to avoid scenes that would make me think. I hardly thought of anything. Nothing crossed my mind. I was playing with my children. My daughter, Elomezino, was on my back while my son, Aghoghomena, was dragging my legs on the floor, but because he was about three years and eight months old then, he could barely drag me owing to my own weight and that of my daughter sitting on my back.

Then I heard the voice of my teacher. "I want to explain something to you" he said. I let my children off me and sat down to hear what He had to say. Love is about lying down to let others sit on you. It is about someone dragging you on the floor. And in all you will accept it as play. Love is really play, if you ask me. No one gets hurt. The joy of play must fill your heart and the hearts of those who are around you. This again points to the principle of acceptance I earlier taught you. Your children are happy to sit on you and to drag you on the floor. This is what everyone you come across want to do to you. They would want to use you as the foundation for their success. Though this is not usually accepted by humans, it is the law that makes heaven peaceful. You are a foundation for another foundation and that foundation is yet for another. This is the principle of continuity. Love is about continuity, bearing the burden of one another, yet with a smile on your face. You bore your daughter's weight and your son tried to bear your own weight and that of his sister. Wouldn't life be sweeter than honey if humans would let this be? I know you weren't expecting me, but you called for this. And I would want you to take down what I have just explained to you. Love is about bearing another's burden without complaint.

"Now, humans come to God every time to pray for a child, and when they have one, they would celebrate and invite everyone to dinner. Years later, they would be the ones to call the child names that would destroy their destinies. Could you imagine a parent calling a child "goat-head?" Isn't that a foolish act? Are children not proof of love? Yes they are. And in like manner, humans have destroyed every good thing that God has given to them. What you call a thing is what it becomes for you. If you want Love to live inside you, think Love only and nothing but Love. Let it envelop your thoughts and acts daily.

DISCOURSE ELEVEN

I remembered ten silly mistakes I had made over the years. I consciously wanted to count up to ten. At the end of that count, I became really sad wondering why I had to make such mistakes when it was obvious that I could have done something better.

The sun was rising from the east and it would surely set in the west. It is natural and nothing would change this fact. This was the thought that was going on in my heart. Then I remembered that my mind had informed my spirit of what I just said and as usual my spirit would surely tell the Holy Spirit, my teacher. My back was aching, but I had no choice but to wait for my teacher to come and teach me. He had often reminded me that I was rather the one troubling Him and that all He does on earth is to teach whoever asks to know about the mystery of life.

I waited, but He didn't show up. I picked up clothing to wear, as it was getting cold outside despite the smile on the face of the sun. Gradually the cold disappeared and the warmth of the sun was sending joy into my nerves. My teacher still had not come. I also knew I should be studying the scriptures now. Within me, I heard a voice saying: "Life is a continuum and nothing is constant, not even the sun and moon. To humans, seasons and times are constants, even the day, but that is not the truth. Everything created by God is dynamic. The cloud is always moving. The wind is also always in motion. The sea waves change. All living creatures grows, even the oldest of humans, animals and trees. The day change ceases, the day the world will end."

Could that voice be my teacher? The voice was deeper than the one that had been teaching me. "It is not the voice of your teacher but that of your mind" the voice replied. "You see, the Holy Spirit has set your mind in a vibrating mode to be able to judge rightly based on the encounter you had earlier with Him. You will now be able to explain the mind of God in the succeeding chapters of this book, because you now have the mind of Christ, due to your desire to learn about Love. Christ is all about Love and nothing more. I am your mind, and will be lending you a helping hand. I work with the principle of replication. I replicate the pattern of your past thoughts on a daily basis and would paint a picture of what your tomorrow would be, because you earlier let me know what you love and cherish. I work with your predominant thought issues. If you refine and renew your mind daily, I won't have to paint disappointments ahead of you."

This is what Love does. It stays refreshed by your thoughts. As long as you do not doubt its existence in your life, it will keep on living in you as though it is a constant. When you refuse to look at the disappointments that came to you as a result of Love, it will keep on painting a picture of a life full of Love in your heart. Now you will also see that since the sun and moon seem to be constant in their path of duty, so also will Love remain constant as you walk through the path of life.

DISCOURSE TWELVE

～

As an author and a teacher of the word of God, the subject of Love has been the central thought of all my discourse, both in my meditations and verbal communications. This has also appeared in various places in my books. It is a push in my heart to explain what has being my understanding about love as presented in my other books:

In my book *Existing in the Supernatural*, which happened to be my first outward proof of my discourse with the spiritual realm, the subject of love opened the book and as one scans through its pages; this is a summary of what one would get:

What defines our relationship with God is love. If we would look around us and see all the provisions which God has put in place – the sun, moon, wind, breeze, animals, your neighbours, etc, and how these provisions have benefitted you, it would be right to say that God loves you more than you love yourself. Many waters cannot quench the love of God for you -Song 8:7. When you see a cloud or the morning dew, ask yourself this question, "Am I faithful to God? Do I really Love Him? Is my Love for God tied to His blessings upon my life?" Check your conscience because that is the beginning of Judgment. Your love for God should not be a bargain service; it should be a wholesome service. This is why we must love those that hate us and keep on forgiven them if we must enlarge our coast. If you don't love God and do His commandment, then you have not truly repented. God gives you authority to inheritance to show His love and care towards you.

This book proves that one thing man owns God is LOVE.

Also if we study through *The Altar in Golgotha*, my second book, resulting from my meditational studies, the subject of LOVE was also given attention:

This book is yet another revelation into the significance of the redemption we received through the cruxification of Jesus Christ, and therefore reminding us of the need to return to God (Isaiah 30:15), who loved us so much that He gave a one off sacrifice to salvage our mutilated souls (John 3:16) from wreck. In effect whatsoever steals our love and submission from God is a devourer. Jacob appreciated love by given his beloved son a coat of many colours. David openly declared how he loved God in 1 Chronicles 21:22-24. Offerings of Gold and Silver are known for their beauty and ornamental value. God required these as offerings in the Old Testament in order to also test submissiveness. This is because since these items are precious, releasing them for God as offering shows that we value God more than those items. God can provide anything for Himself if he so wanted to. He does this because He wants a constant relationship and a demonstration of love from man. If we show love to one another, it shows that we truly love God. In songs 8:6 the Bible says that love is as strong as death, and that Jealousy is as cruel as the grave. Jealousy is the enemy of love. In John 15:12 Christ made us to know that we must love one another because this is the ingredient the world is lacking, the reason for every problem we are having. A demonstration of this Altar show of love is what Christ explained in Matthew 25:35-40, which could be summarised as CARE. We must stop gossip and backbiting. Every true believer must avoid evil and seek after love........

We would see that this book treats Love as due diligence of service unto God and care for our neighbours.

Yet another of my spiritual discourses was contained in another book. *Battles Beyond the Physical* started on this note: "The Bible, in 1 Corinthians 2:9, says that we are destined for a greater reward if only we can love God. This can be confirmed with what Joshua experienced in Joshua 6:27: '*So the Lord was with Joshua; and his fame was noised throughout all the country.*'" And followed through to talk about love as follows:

The book of Romans 8:38-39 says that nothing can separate us from the love of God. What, then, is the love of God? Why can't we love God so that we can stop all the complaints of dissatisfaction around us? Saint Paul, in 1 Corinthians 2:7, says that the secrets to understanding the love of God are hidden in mysteries which existed from the foundation of the world. And these secrets are found in the word (John 1:1) which is the Lamb that was slain on the day the foundation of this earth was laid (Revelation 13:8), and in that emptiness (Genesis 1:1-2), the everlasting foundation of truth stood tall as a living testimony of the eternal love of God towards all of us (1 Corinthians 3:11, 2 Timothy 2:19). Once we can love God, he will reward us (Hebrew 11:6). This reward was further explained, in Revelation 5:3, to be only for those who overcome. When we love God, we become like the sun in its fullness of heat (Judges 5:31), with an angel leading us (Exodus 23:20), who stands in the sun (Revelations 19:17) and ensures the sun obeyed the voice of Gideon (Judges 7), and also made the sun stand still for Joshua to enable him to put God's enemies to shame (Joshua 10:13). This implies that our love for God is what equips us daily for the unseen battles we fight on earth.

We would see that this book sees our strength in spiritual battles as a product of our love for God.

More on the subject of Love would be seen also in another of my books, *The Path to Absolute Freedom*, while sailing through the sea of spiritual knowledge and understanding about the pains in this world:

What have many of us done? This is also captured in John 3 Verse 19 when Jesus says that people love darkness instead of light, because their deeds were evil. We are loved by God, and God cannot plot evil against us, because "God is good all the time." If we truly loved our neighbour as we love ourselves, we wouldn't have enemies around us. God is ever interested in our eternal wellbeing, because it gives Him joy. Anything the devil hates is what we must love. Devil hates marriage, but loves sexual immoralities outside marriage, so we must do otherwise. The devil hates people living together in peace and harmony, so we must live in peace. Those who are in the world love oral and anal sex, for instance, so we must avoid oral and anal sex – whether in marriage or outside marriage.

Yet in this book, Love is seen as walking in light, being at peace with everyone and rejecting whatever makes the devil happy.

I wasn't yet satisfied with what I had known as what Love has to offer. This led me into another meditational discourse and wrote down my encounter in yet another book, *The Man God Made*. Here is what I got:

God's beloved new friends abandon Him and follow His enemy to travel through the sea of pleasure and worldly treasures. There and then, God sits down, waiting patiently for His Spirit to woo another to Him, who will inherit His large kingdom with a song. While the search is going on, the Angels are singing, but God refuses to be moved by their songs. The usual smile in His face has disappeared. His heart sings a song as He looks through the heart of men:

Love me, if you can -
You are the one I love;
Don't you run away from me,
I am still waiting for you.

Lack of love is characterised by envy, jealousy, hatred, backbiting, covetousness and the likes. Love is about care. It is about provision for the needy in our midst. Before we became born again, we were sinners, and now that we have Christ in our lives, if we truly love sinners the way Christ did, we would become effective soul winners, through the show of charity within our neighbourhood...

I could sense the subject of Love becoming clearer in my heart. This discourse summarises Love as returning back to God, loving sinners the way Christ did as a means of soul winning, and then showing that we care through welfare service.

Should I say I was satisfied? Well so it seemed, but I wanted to learn more until I saw the same reasoning overlapping in my thought process. Then I would know that I have understood the subject of Love, the reason God gave His only begotten son to redeem mankind from sin.

This quest for more knowledge gave birth to another book, this time on the subject of love in marriage, which is the most popular love institution humans know. The book was titled *Aspects of Marriage*. Let's see what we would learn:

The husband and wife are to complement and honour one another. As God's instruments of peace, they are supposed to be dedicated to the service of God all the days of their lives, in love. To love means to release and yield the substance of strength in you to the recipient. The love a man has for his children is normally an extension of that which he has for his wife. The phrase 'I love you' is a vow and an oath before God who was the secret witness. To love a man means to yield and submit to him, or to be 'loyal to his government', so to say. The marital vows you make, the rings both of you wear, the togetherness you share on the undefiled bed, the sweet names you call yourselves etc, are enough evidence of the love you share. I once defined love as 'Life Of Veritable Evidence (LOVE)'. The veritability in the life both of you share together is your first point of exploration......

Obviously, this book talks about submission, loyalty, humility, sacrifice, oaths, vows, etc, and every home that doesn't breed love would bring forth children who would turn society upside down – they often become the hooligans wherever we tend to make a living.

While I thought I was having a better grasp of the subject now, this was when I went into another meditation mode. This time it was to ponder the subject of leadership, and of course, Love found its way into the book. Here is what the book, *Leadership – An Eagle Eye Perspective*, has to say about the subject of Love:

To love is to care. There is no one who senses this act in a leader that would not be ready to lend a helping hand to his vision. A leader with the heart that loves will always experience love blossoming among those he leads. People love God and want to serve Him, so any leader who sacrifices in building a house of worship and fellowship unto God is bound to succeed. The Centurion was recommended to Jesus as one deserving God's intervention when his servant was sick in Luke 7:2-6 when they said... "for he loves our nation, and has built us a synagogue."

In the course of writing this book on leadership, the obvious truth that kept resounding within me was the fact that leadership breeds on love, to God and to mankind, and that, to a large extent, love has a lot to do with how we fear God and carry out His instructions in leading His children wherever leadership is at work.

It was time to understand the interplay between the anointing and love, and it was the subject of another meditation. This led to another book, *Gifted and Anointed*. In this book the subject of love resonated into the fabric of existence and I noted:

Life is not about noisy prayers or the expectation of miracles, but about adding value to the lives of those we meet daily – this is the essence of the love of God we share. And with the anointing you can do this onerous task of humanity better. If you are the type who loves little children, and they easily comes around you, then you will definitely succeed in life. What you love is what lives in you. Love what God loves to remain relevant.

This book pointed us to the basis of the anointing of God upon any one which is to exercise the gift of Love.

Our lives on earth depend on love.

DISCOURSE
THIRTEEN

Now I conclude that Love is the essence of living. We have seen Love in various dimensions visiting and nourishing the earth and all that dwells in it, but we may not have realised it. When Love wants to bring comfort and abundance, it comes in the form of rain. When it is time to give us warmth, Love becomes the rays of the sun. In the night Love turns to the moon to give us light. Are you hot and need cooling? Love turns to breeze. Are you lonely and want some companionship? Love becomes the songs of birds through your window. When you are disappointed and weighed down, Love becomes the smiles on the faces of babies. So we can see that Love lives.

For every question I have asked in my meditations, all the answers have pointed to one expression of life, and that is LOVE. Love purifies and sanctifies. It is the ensign of heavenly glory seen in God's creation. It is the totality of the presence of God on earth, and it is all around us, if only we would try to seek it all the days of our lives. Love is natural. Love is pretty. Love is daring fear and failure. Love soars like the eagles and perches like the butterflies. Love distinguishes men and women of integrity, and establishes them. Love binds our hearts to every object of beauty and simulates reality in our thoughts. Love brings hope to the hopeless and sends joy into a mourning heart. Love creates emotional balance in us. Love triggers the hormones in our body into action. Love brings forth life, always and always.

And don't forget this – A man's ego kills the spark of Love in him, and a deceitful life buries it. Communication paves the way for Love and the spirit of appreciation beautifies Love.

And, finally I have this to say – God is Love, and if we would look behind the words of Revelation 5:12, we would see that the fruits of Love are seen as power, riches, wisdom, strength, honour, glory and blessing. And all these would represent God's intention for mankind:

27 So God created man in his own image, in the image of God he created him; male and female he created them.

28 God blessed them and said to them, "Be fruitful and increase in number; fill the earth and subdue it. Rule over the fish of the

sea and the birds of the air and over every living creature that moves
on the ground."

29 Then God said, "I give you every seed-bearing plant on the face
of the whole earth and every tree that has fruit with seed in it. They
will be yours for food.

30 And to all the beasts of the earth and all the birds of the air and
all the creatures that move on the ground everything that has the
breath of life in it- I give every green plant for food." **And it was**
so. - Genesis 1:27-30.

The last statement above says, "And it was so." This is what
explains the Love of God towards mankind. We just have to
walk our way back to God so that this decree will appear in
our lives. I leave this last word with you:

LOVE DOESN'T STRUGGLE TO LIVE; IT IS ALWAYS THERE.

IT IS THE ESSENCE OF LIVING.

COVENANT
CONFESSION

If you are not born again, you may have read this book as literary material and will not receive the spirit it carries. You can make a decision to correct that now by saying this covenant confession: Lord Jesus, I know now that you died for my sins. I believe and confess you as my Lord and Saviour. Please come into my life and dwell inside of me. If you just said this confession, you should locate a spirit filled church to fellowship with them – let the pastor know you just gave your life to Christ and you will be directed on what to do next. Salvation is a personal race and you must be serious with it.

You can also call us through the numbers below: +234-8076190064; +234-8086737791. Or send us an email at: christmovementinternational@gmail.com

BOOKS BY THE SAME AUTHOR

1. Existing In The Supernatural

2. The Altar In Golgotha

3. How Good and Large is your Land?

4. Born To Blossom

5. Battles Beyond The Physical

6. The Path To Absolute Freedom

7. The Man God Made

8. Aspects of Marriage

9. Leadership – An Eagle-Eye Perspective

10. Gifted and Anointed

11. The Subject of Love – A Discourse

About the Author

Pastor Oghenethoja Umuteme encountered God the day he was baptised at the St Stephen's Anglican Church, Owhelogbo Delta State, when he received a warm feeling in his heart as he confessed the Lord Jesus as His lord and personal saviour. His birth was surrounded with mysteries – he was born to a mother who had been barren for 8 years. There was hardly anything he said that did not come to pass as he was growing. In 1994 he had a dream in which he received an orange which contained a bible with a red cover. Events continued dramatically until he started hearing voices telling him to go for rescue, as many souls were heading for destruction. Then it became clear to him that he was being called to carry out the task of restoring mankind back to Jesus. In January 2006, he heard a voice telling him to read Isaiah 42. On reading to verse 6, he felt a deep force within him and started trembling and a voice said - 'I have called you'. As he read further he was getting immersed in the spirit of God and when he read verse 22, the voice said, 'this is your task'. Then on the 13th of October 2008, he heard a voice while driving: 'Service starts in your house on Sunday.' Events happened that were beyond his understanding and on Sunday 19th October 2008, the first public worship service came to pass.

Pastor Oghenethoja Umuteme is a prolific writer and oversees a leadership foundation, Umuteme Leadership Foundation, which he uses to teach good leadership and a School of Ministry to empower church leaders. A member of the Nigerian Society of Engineers, he is currently, as at the time of publishing this book, a practising Engineering Design Lead with over ten years work experience in the oil and gas industry in different pipeline engineering functions – design, procurement, fabrication, construction, integrity management, maintenance and operation. A gospel musician with a recorded album, Breaking Through, he is also the Founder and Senior Pastor at Royal Diamonds International Church, Port Harcourt, Nigeria. He is an established teacher of the word of God and a prophet to the nation, as shown by his books. Using his crusade ministry – Giant Strides World Outreach Crusade - Pst. Oghenethoja reaches people with the undiluted word of salvation. And as a prophet to the nations, he has declared prophecies that have been fulfilled – the latest one being the famine that will visit the earth for ten years starting from the year 2017 and ending in 2027. He is also a man of miracles with testimonies said by those who have benefited from the gift of God in his life. As a motivational preacher, he has encouraged many to become successful in their chosen careers. The books God has used him to write has brought healing and encouraged many all over the world with testimonies sent to his email box. These books have also been used as teaching and counselling materials by many, including pastors. His wife, Mrs. Umuteme Adokiye Obele, who supports him in this call of God upon his life has borne him children.

www.ingramcontent.com/pod-product-compliance
Lightning Source LLC
Chambersburg PA
CBHW060144050426
42448CB00010B/2289